D1486975

Diving

Tony Norman

GARETH**STEVENS**

PUBLISHING

A Member of the WRC Media Family of Companies

Please visit our web site at: **www.garethstevens.com**
For a free color catalog describing Gareth Stevens Publishing's
list of high-quality books and multimedia programs, call
1-800-542-2595 (USA) or **1-800-387-3178** (Canada).
Gareth Stevens Publishing's fax: (414) 332-3567.

Library of Congress Cataloging-in-Publication Data

Norman, Tony.
    Diving / Tony Norman.
        p. cm. — (Action sports)
    ISBN 0-8368-6367-4 (lib. bdg.)
    1. Diving—Juvenile literature. I. Title. II. Action sports (Milwaukee, Wis.)
    GV838.613.N67   2006
    797.2'3—dc22   2005053683

This edition first published in 2006 by
Gareth Stevens Publishing
A Member of the WRC Media Family of Companies
330 West Olive Street, Suite 100
Milwaukee, Wisconsin 53212 USA

This U.S. edition copyright © 2006 by Gareth Stevens, Inc. Original
edition copyright © 2006 by ticktock Entertainment Ltd. First published in
2006 by ticktock Media Ltd., Unit 2, Orchard Business Centre, North Farm Road,
Tunbridge Wells, Kent TN2 3XF, U.K.

Gareth Stevens editor: Carol Ryback
Gareth Stevens designer: Scott M. Krall

Picture credits: (t)=top; (b)=bottom; (c)=center; (l)=left; (r)=right
CORBIS: 20(c). Desert Divers: www.desert-divers.com 29(b). FPLA: 25(bl), 25(b),
25(br); / Frank W. Lane 13(bcr); / Colin Marshall 12(br), 13(bl); / D. P. Wilson 13(br);
/ Minden Pictures: / Fred Bavendam 13(bcl); / Norbert Wu 22(b). The Florida Tourist
Board: 29(br). Montana Miller: 8(c). NASA: 26(cr). National Undersea Research
Program (NURP): / OAR 27(b), 27(br). NOAA: 24(c), 28(br), 29(ttr), 29(tcr); / Liz
Baird 26(br); / Ocean Explorer 25(bl), 26(tr). Red Bull®: / © Stefan Aufschnaiter 6(c);
/ © Bernhard Spöttel 9(t); / © Mark Watson 5(bl), 7(t), 7(cr). Science Photo Library: /
Gregory Ochocki 25(t). Stockbyte: 4(bl), 5(br), 5(tcl), 5(tr), 15(t), 17(t), 18(c), 19(t),
22(c), 23(t). Whale Watch South Africa: / Yvonne Kamp 11(t), 12(c). White Shark
Diving Company: / Marion Ritter 10(c), 13(t).

Every effort has been made to trace the copyright holders, and we apologize
in advance for any unintentional omissions. We will be pleased to insert the
appropriate acknowledgments in any subsequent edition of this publication.

Printed in the United States of America

1 2 3 4 5 6 7 8 9 10 09 08 07 06

Contents

Introduction

The oceans have always fascinated humans. Today, more than twelve million people dive from cliffs or explore coral reefs, ice caves, underwater forests, and blue holes. Scientist divers in submersibles explore depths of more than 36,000 feet (11,000 meters).

Cliffs and cages

Cliff divers perform an ancient ritual in front of large tourist audiences. Cage divers throw a mixture of fish parts and blood (called "chum") into the ocean. The chum attracts sharks and other fish as caged divers wait for a close-up view.

With ice or without?

Ice divers cut holes in frozen inland lakes or in the ice packs of the polar regions. Insulated dry suits help the divers stay warm in the icy-cold waters. Divers exploring the warmer waters off Australia's Great Barrier Reef wear regular wet suits. The Great Barrier Reef (GBR) began forming more than eight thousand years ago. The GBR is now a rich marine habitat.

Divers may encounter huges schools of colorful fish on a reef.

Diving facts – **Did you know?**

Oceans contain 97 percent of Earth's water and cover 70 percent of Earth's surface. Ocean water temperatures average 39 °Fahrenheit (4 °Celsius) — just above freezing.

Cage Diving

Scuba Diving

Ice Diving

Deep-Sea Diving

The leafy sea dragon lives in the waters south and west of Australia.

A clownfish, or anemonefish, peeks out from an anemone.

Cliff Diving

Cliff divers jump from heights of 80–115 feet (25 to 35 m). Each dive lasts about three seconds. The divers spin and twist in the air, then hit the water at more than 60 miles (100 km) per hour. Most divers land feetfirst to reduce the risk of injury.

Brave hearts

Cliff diving began on the Hawaiian island of Lanai. Warriors jumped from the cliffs to show their bravery. They used a rock ledge 85 feet (26 m) above the ocean. The World Cliff Diving Championships are sometimes held at the same site.

Top hot spot

Cliff divers in Acapulco, Mexico, perform in daily tourist shows. They wait for high tide, when the water at the foot of the cliffs rises from 2 feet (60 centimeters) to 12 feet (365 cm).

Competitive divers hope to enter the water with barely a splash.

Diving facts – Did you know?

Cliff divers hit the water feetfirst. They fall so fast and hard that they could break a foot — or even a leg — if a fish or a piece of seaweed gets in their way.

World champion cliff diver Joey Zuber, from Queensland, Australia, flips off a cliff in Kimberley, Western Australia.

TRUE STORIES

Wolfgangsee, Austria, 2005. American diver Daniel Ballarin made cliff diving history when he did the first-ever five-somersault dive in competition from an 88-foot (27-m) cliff.

Mazatlan, in western Mexico, is popular with cliff divers.

Cliff divers jump into freshwater lakes as well as the ocean.

Divers look for rocky outcroppings above deep water.

No Place for Fear

Danger is part of cliff diving. Divers lessen their fear by being well prepared for diving. Professional cliff divers always plan ahead for dive competitions or performances.

The dive zone

The "dive zone" is the area where the divers enter the water. They check for rocks or other obstacles in the waters below the cliffs. Before competitons, they warm up with stretching and other mild exercises — while focusing their minds on their first dives.

Show time

Every dive tests divers' nerves and skills. As divers stand at the top of a cliff, they focus on the dive zones below. Divers rise up on their toes before diving off the cliffs and into thin air. They turn, twist, and spin to enter the water feetfirst. A diver is in the air for just a few seconds before hitting the water.

Montana Miller was one of the first women to dive from the cliffs of Acupulco, Mexico.

Diving facts – **Did you know?**

How high are the cliff dives? The world's best cliff divers take off from cliffs that are three times higher than the highest diving boards in the Olympic Games.

Dubrovnik, Croatia, is an increasingly popular cliff-diving site.

TRUE STORIES

Mexico 1976. Pat Sucher of Dayton, Ohio, became the first American to win the Acapulco Cliff Diving Championships. He got a perfect score of ten points in all five rounds.

Cliff divers enter the Ionian Sea from the island of Corfu, Greece.

Cliff divers avoid landing on their back or chest.

Cliff diving does not require special equipment.

Acapulco, Mexico, is a popular cliff-diving site.

Cage Diving

One of the most thrilling ways to see great white sharks up close is through the bars of a steel dive cage. Divers stay inside the cage while the sharks swim free around them, often attacking the cage with their mighty jaws.

Best dives

The best places to see great white sharks include the waters off South Africa, South Australia, Mexico, and California. Expert teams run the shark cage diving trips.

Blood in the water

Crew members on the cage-diving boat throw "chum" — an oily, mushy mix of fish parts and blood — into the ocean to attract the sharks, which are drawn in by the smell of blood in the water. When the sharks appear, the cage divers climb into the cage, the lid is shut tight, and the cage is lowered into the water. A strong nylon rope tethers the cage to the boat. Divers watch as sharks surround and even attack the cage, which floats a short distance from the boat.

Great white sharks eat fish, squid, other sharks, whales, dolphins, and sea lions — and have been known to attack people.

Diving facts - Did you know?

Great white sharks must swim constantly or they will sink. Sharks can smell a single drop of blood in 26 gallons (100 liters) of water.

Adult great white sharks measure 13 to 19 feet (4 to 5 m) long.

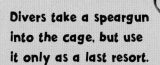

Divers take a speargun into the cage, but use it only as a last resort.

Chum is an oily mush of fish parts. Some chum comes in packages.

Most cage divers record their shark encounter with an underwater camera.

Shark's Teeth

Diving cages are small but strong enough to withstand the fury of a shark attack. Divers wear wet suits, boots, gloves, and masks. They also wear weights that help them stand and balance in the cage while underwater.

Inside the dive cage

Divers must stay still inside the diving cage. Great whites swim right up to the bars. Divers are forbidden from trying to touch the animals. The sharks are dangerous wild predators that can rip apart flesh.

Right or wrong?

Some people think cage diving is wrong. They believe it encourages sharks to link humans to food and increases the number of shark attacks. Cage divers say there is no proof that this is true. They say cage diving is a unique opportunity to get a closer view of sharks.

A shark's dorsal and caudal fins stick out above the water when the shark is near the surface.

Diving facts - Did you know?

Only about twelve of the nearly 400 shark species are dangerous to humans, with three species responsible for most of the attacks. Every year, about ten people die from shark attacks — but humans kill 100 million sharks annually.

Great white sharks have about three thousand teeth arranged in several rows.

TRUE STORIES

San Francisco, Califonia, 2002. A shark jumped from the water and onto the beach to attack surfer Lee Fontan on the back and leg. Fontan needed one hundred stitches to close his wounds.

Most sharks are fairly small: the coral cat shark is only 24 inches (60cm) long.

A hammerhead shark, with eyes on either side of its oddly shaped head, has good vision.

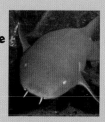

Nurse sharks sometimes live in groups in shallow waters.

Scuba Diving

Scuba divers take an air supply underwater with them. They carry a cylinder on their back filled with compressed air. The air lasts as long as one hour if the diver does not dive too deep.

First lessons

Some divers learn to scuba dive as early as age twelve. Scuba students learn about diving equipment, skills, and techniques. The lessons include classroom lectures and written tests, as well as exercises in swimming pools and open-water sessions.

The Sardine Run

The Sardine Run, along the coast of South Africa, is a spectacular scuba diving experience. Every winter, millions of sardines swim north toward warmer waters. So many fish move at once that they are visible by satellite. The Sardine Run becomes a feeding frenzy for dolphins, fur seals, whales, and many shark species. Scuba divers can get close-up views as the sardines twist and turn like huge silver clouds under the water.

A diving cylinder contains the same mixture of gases that make up surface air. The diver breathes the air through a regulator.

Diving facts - Did you know?

Scuba divers can watch the dolphins hunting during the Sardine Run. The dolphins force the shoals of fish into a ball shape, then close in for a feast of sardines.

TRUE STORIES

Marine biologist Andrew Aitkin studies the Sardine Run. "We don't really know why they do it," he says. "It is not a true migration . . . the sardines do not travel for feeding or breeding."

Scuba diving flippers help divers move through the water more efficiently.

Okay?

stop

out of air

ears not clearing

Scuba's Mega Mix

Australia's Great Barrier Reef is one of the world's best and most famous scuba diving sites. It consists of more than two thousand smaller coral reefs. Other important coral reefs are in the Caribbean Sea, the Red Sea, and Polynesia.

A living thing

The centuries-old Great Barrier Reef is so big that it is visible from space. More than 1,500 fish species, 500 seaweed species, and 400 coral species live on the GBR. Coral grows at only about 1/2 inch (1 to 2cm) per year.

Kelp "forests"

Kelp is a large seaweed that looks like underwater trees. Kelp grows as tall as 130 feet (40 m) from the seabed. Sea otters, seals, sea lions, snails, crabs, jellyfish, and other marine creatures live in the kelp beds off California's coast. Great white sharks also hang around kelp forests. Whales, sea horses, and rock lobsters call Tasmania's kelp forests home.

Sea turtles spend most of their lives in the open ocean, coming onto land only to lay their eggs.

Diving facts - Did you know?

Male sea horses become "pregnant." After mating, the male carries the young and gives birth to about fifty babies at one time.

Coral reefs grow in sunny, clear water to depths of about 300 feet (100 m).

TRUE STORIES

Australia 1998. Two U.S. scuba divers died in the shark-filled seas of the Great Barrier Reef. A tourist dive boat left them behind by mistake. Their bodies were never found.

boat

watch me

check your depth

find your buddy

Blue Holes

Blue holes are found in the Caribbean Sea and around the Bahamas. They began as caves on dry land, then filled with ocean water millions of years ago. Over time, the roofs of the caves collapsed and formed the blue holes.

Secrets of the deep

Dives into blue holes can last an hour or longer. Divers use double air tanks and link themselves together with safety ropes. They carry one main dive light and two backup lights. A thicker than normal wet suit helps protect against the cold water. Like most scuba divers, blue hole divers also use dive computers that keep track of depth, time, and air supply.

Larger fish living in deep-water caves show no fear of people.

Belize mystery

The Great Blue Hole, near Belize, is one of the best dives in the world. The Hole measures 1,000 feet (305 m) wide and 412 feet (125 m) deep. Many tunnels lead off from the main part of the Great Blue Hole. Scuba divers mapped some of these tunnels, but many remain unexplored.

Diving facts - Did you know?

The Great Blue Hole is known as one of the world's best shark dives. The shark species include hammerhead, bull, lemon, tiger, and black-tip reef sharks.

Cave divers take advanced training and use special equipment to explore an underwater world few people ever see.

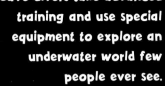

TRUE STORIES

In the Bahamas, local legends tell of the "lusca" who live in the blue holes. Half dragon and half squid, these evil creatures pull swimmers deep underwater to their deaths.

Cave divers should always dive in pairs - never alone.

Many unique plants and animals live in the deepest caves.

Cave divers follow the light back to the exit.

Ice Diving

Ice divers must stay warm. They wear special exposure suits called dry suits with a thick thermal layer underneath to protect against the icy temperatures. Divers also wear insulated hoods, gloves, and full face masks to conserve body heat.

Hard water

Divers cut a hole in the ice using pick axes or chain saws. Before entering the water, the ice divers connect ropes to their bodies. Safety divers who stay on the ice's surface tend the other end of the rope. The divers signal how the dive is going by tugging on the rope. Safety divers stay ready to enter the water and provide assistance if needed. Most ice dives last only about twenty minutes.

Ice caves

Under the ice, the ocean glows in shades of blue and green. The smooth walls of underwater ice tunnels look as if they are made of colored glass.

Scientists study the ice, penguins, and the oceans around Antarctica. They also do research in the Arctic.

Diving facts - **Did you know?**

Ice divers in Canada's Arctic Bay may encounter polar bears. Half of the thirty thousand polar bears left in the world live in Canada.

TRUE STORIES

American Bob Wass, Australian Brett Cormick, and Austrian Michael Wolff became the first international team to dive under the Arctic ice at the North Pole during the 1999 North Pole Expedition.

Most ice diving for fun occurs in frozen inland lakes. Divers who explore the icy waters of the Arctic or around Antarctica are usually scientists.

An ice pick helps divers break through the ice.

Dry suits protect ice divers from freezing.

Thick ice diving gloves let divers grip gear.

A diver needs to use a flashlight in the dim light under the ice.

Deep-Sea Diving

Most recreational scuba diving in the oceans occurs in shallow waters near land. Working divers and diving scientists who visit deeper waters need specialized training and equipment. Water pressure becomes stronger the deeper a diver goes. Deep-sea divers need protection from this crushing force.

Deep-sea workers

Deep-sea working divers wear special pressure suits with metal helmets and leaded boots. They stay linked to their boats at all times. The link supplies air, power for lighting, and a way to talk to people on the surface.

Space-age dive suits

A "JIM suit" looks like a space suit with big bendy arms, metal hands, and a clear dome for a helmet. Power boosters help the diver move along the bottom in the great pressures of extreme depths — down to 2,000 feet (600 m). The suit weighs 1,000 pounds (450 kilograms) and has its own air supply.

The spotted ratfish lives in the dark, icy depths at 2,900 feet (900 m).

Diving facts - Did you know?

Divers who come to the surface too fast from a dive risk getting decompression sickness, or "the bends," which can cause joint pain, dizzy spells, and or even paralysis.

Professional divers soemtimes explore and salvage deep ocean wrecks.

TRUE STORIES

The deepest human dive occurred in the Mariana Trench near Guam in 1960. The two-person *Trieste* bathyscaphe descended to 35,798 feet (10,911 m) for about twenty minutes. This record still stands.

Divers often wear thick, thermal underwear underneath a dry suit.

The one-piece, watertight dry suit often has padded knees and seat.

A woman's dry suit is cut to fit a female body.

Divers need a pressure-proof watch to keep track of time.

Monsters of the Deep

No light shines in the deepest parts of the ocean. Strange fish and other marine creatures live in these dark waters. Humans are just beginning to explore the great depths.

Weird world

A giant squid can grow up to 65 feet (20 m) long. It catches and holds prey using the large suckers on its ten legs. A quick bite from the squid's sharp beak kills its prey. Vampire squid live as deep as 3,000 feet (900 m) and have a light-producing organ in their body that can blink on and off. Sharp spikes make the vampire squid look like something out of a space movie!

Into the future

The United States plans to launch a new deep-sea submersible in 2008. It will be able to reach depths of more than 21,000 feet (6,500 m) and will help explore more than 99 percent of the world's seabed.

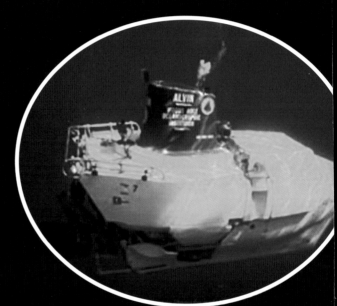

For more than forty years, scientists have used the submersible, ALVIN, to explore the ocean depths.

Diving facts - **Did you know?**

Deep-water hagfish dig into the flesh of other fish, then eat them alive from the inside out.

The fangtooth has a short body, large head, and long teeth. Luckily it is only 6 inches (15cm) long.

TRUE STORIES

Sperm whales hunt and eat giant squid. The whales take big breaths before diving deep to catch their prey. Some whales can stay underwater for almost an hour.

The black sea dragon has a fishing lure in front of its mouth to attract prey.

The deep-sea anglerfish has a bioluminescent light at the end of its nose lure.

The hinged mouth of the deep-sea gulper swings open wide to swallow large prey.

Brave Hearts

Thousands of years ago, Hawaiian warriors dived off cliffs into the ocean to prove they had no fear. Modern deep-sea explorers may not dive from cliffs, but they still need plenty of courage for their adventures.

House underwater

Early in her career, pioneering marine biologist Sylvia Earle lived 50 feet (15 m) under the ocean for two weeks to study ocean habitats. In 1979, Sylvia set a world record for the deepest solo dive: 1,250 feet (381 m), and has logged at least 6,000 hours underwater. She currently works for the National Geographic Society.

Old man of the sea

French explorer Jacques-Yves Cousteau helped invent the Aqua-Lung. The Cousteau television programs brought the oceans into living rooms around the globe and made millions aware of the wonders of the ocean environment.

The TITANIC, as seen today.

Jacques-Yves Cousteau was world-famous for his decades of diving experience and his efforts to teach others about ocean life.

Marine biologist Sylvia Earle writes books about ocean environments.

Diving facts - Did you know?

Explorer Robert Ballard made more than sixty-five missions in deep-dive submersibles. In 1985, he found the historic wreck of the TITANIC in the North Atlantic.

TRUE STORIES

France 2004. Loic Leferme set the free-diving world record. He took one deep breath and went down to 560 feet (171 m). The entire dive took 3 minutes and 40 seconds.

The hard dive suit allows divers to work at depths of 1,000 feet (305 m).

Professional divers include scientists and underwater construction workers.

Sylvia Earle holds a sea creature.

Sylvia prepares for a dive in a JIM suit.

Map of the Oceans

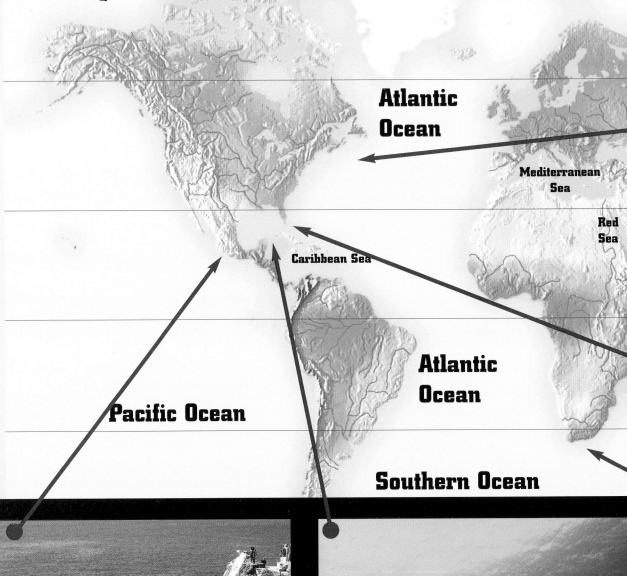

Atlantic Ocean

Mediterranean Sea

Red Sea

Caribbean Sea

Atlantic Ocean

Pacific Ocean

Southern Ocean

Cliff diving in Acapulco, Mexico.

Diving near Belize's Great Blue Hole in the Caribbean Sea.

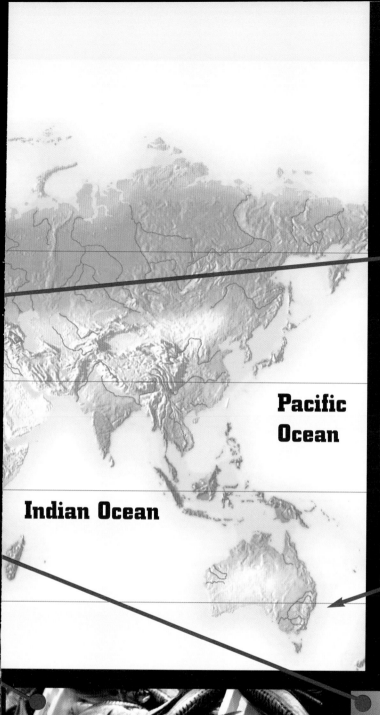

Pacific Ocean

Indian Ocean

Wreck of the *Titanic*.

Australia's Great Barrier Reef.

South Africa's Sardine Run is a great opportunity for local people to enjoy fresh fish.

Exploring a shipwreck in the Florida Keys.

Glossary

anemones: sea animals with soft tentacles; they stay in one place and often resemble flowers.

Aqua-Lung: diving equipment that includes an air cylinder and a device that regulates the pressure at which air enters a diver's lungs.

bathyscaphe: a deep-sea submersible.

bioluminescence: the light produced by chemical reactions within a living creature.

blue holes: deep underwater caves with collapsed roofs.

caudal fin: tail fin.

chum: fishy mixture thrown into the ocean to attract sharks and other fish.

compressed: squeezed to fit into a smaller than normal area.

coral: skeletons of tiny marine animals called polyps that form rock-like deposits over thousands of years, usually near the shoreline.

coral reef: a large area of coral that provides a habitat for other marine life.

cylinder: a diving tank that contains compressed air.

dive computers: electronic instruments that keep track of depths, time, and amount of air remaining in cylinder.

dive zone: the target area in which a cliff diver hopes to enter the water.

dorsal fin: a back fin.

dry suit: a diving suit that keeps a diver dry and somewhat warm in cold water.

ear clearing: "popping" of the ears to relieve internal air pressure within the head upon descent.

feeding frenzy: the wild, frantic actions of many animals, all trying to eat the same food at the same time.

flippers: fin-shaped footwear that helps divers swim more efficiently.

freshwater: water that is not salty.

free diving: extreme, breath-holding, deep diving done with only a mask, fins, and snorkel.

great white: the largest species of shark; found in all oceans.

hard dive suit: a diving suit with a metal helmet and weighted shoes; often used by underwater construction workers.

high tide: the highest of the varying water levels of an ocean.

inland lakes: large bodies of freshwater surrounded by land.

insulated: protected against heat or cold.

JIM suit: a reinforced diving suit that protects the diver from extreme water pressure at depths while out of a submersible.

kelp: a large, fast-growing seaweed.

marine biologist: a scientist who specializes in studying ocean-related subjects.

migration: the (often seasonal) movement of animals to a different geographic location, usually for feeding or mating.

open water: a natural body of water, such as an ocean, lake, or river.

paralysis: the inability to move ones' limbs.

predator: an animal that catches and eats other animals.

recreational: for fun.

regulator: a device that adjusts the pressure coming from a tank of compressed air.

salvage: to gather and reuse.

satellite: a space-based orbiting device that monitors conditions on Earth.

species: a unique animal or plant.

shoals: large groups of fish that move together.

tank: another word for a dive cylinder.

submersible (submarine, or sub): an underwater craft that can travel to and withstand the water pressure at great depths.

tethers: the ropes, lines, or hoses that link a diver to the surface.

thermal: having to do with heat.

Titanic: a ship that sank after hitting an iceberg during its maiden voyage in April 1912.

warm up: slowly getting one's muscles used to movement to avoid injury.

wet suit: a tight, rubber suit that traps a layer of water against the skin to help keep a diver warm.

Index